My Son, My Son
Anti-depressants, Suicide, Comfort

Evelyn Hinds

My Son, My Son

Copyright © 2014 Evelyn Hinds

All rights reserved.

ISBN:1502571730
ISBN-13: 978-1502571731

My Son, My Son

CONTENTS

1	Introduction	Pg 1
2	Precious Memories	Pg 3
3	Psalm 139	Pg 5
4	The Call	Pg 7
5	His Chair	Pg 9
6	The Grave	Pg 11
7	Let Wes Speak	Pg 13
8	Making a Difference	Pg 17
9	Sanctity of Life	Pg 21
10	No Clues	Pg 23
11	Preparations	Pg 27
12	Quotes	Pg 29
13	The Photo	Pg 31
14	The Timing	Pg 35
15	The Service	Pg 37
16	A Poem	Pg 41
17	Comfort	Pg 43
18	The Video	Pg 45
19	Sharing	Pg 47
20	Treasures	Pg 49
21	Gold	Pg 53
22	Dr. Breggin	Pg 69
23	Gratitude	Pg 73
24	Epilogue	Pg 77

Introduction

Death of a child is any mother's nightmare. No one would choose this journey but it was chosen for me. It's something I have not gotten over nor do I ever expect to. Pain that deep leaves a scar. In my dreams about my son he's alive. I wake up to the truth but I'm happy that I had time with him again. My journey is teaching me to practice taking my focus off my loss and seeing with grateful eyes the years that came before my son's last moments on earth.

John Wesley Czarnota was called Wes by his family but the rest of the world called him John. I often just called him "my son, my son." I would use different inflections to communicate my mood. He liked that. On his thirty-seventh birthday, one month before his passing, he marveled, "Ma, can you believe it, I'm almost forty." It was hard for me to believe, time had flown by!

Wes was my only child. I had a deep-seated desire in me to have children. My mother modeled the joy of being a mother. I'd always thought I'd have two children but life did not cooperate with me on that. I had three miscarriages trying to fulfill that dream. But I did have Wes and even I didn't realize how much I could love and enjoy a child. He was delightful.

Shortly before Wes' fourth birthday, he was diagnosed with neurofibromatosis. We were told that it was a rare condition that he had since birth. It could have many manifestations and could be life-threatening. He was diagnosed and treated in Switzerland, at Boston Massachusetts General Hospital, and at K. U. Med Center in our hometown of Kansas City. My heart was shattered. I cried for years and that is not much of an exaggeration. However, as Wes grew up, he needed less treatment. As an adult, he lived most of his years with no medication or treatment. I've learned this condition was from A-Z, it could be benign or it could have many complications. Still, because of this diagnosis, I lived more keenly aware than most mothers that tomorrow is not promised.

Wes' father and I divorced when Wes was five but we both lived in the same town until I moved out of state when Wes was nineteen. We had "joint custody." Wes and I were always very close and when he was with his father he called me every day. That practice continued in adulthood so I talked with him nearly every day of his life. His dad saw him more often than I did since he lived only a few miles from him but they didn't visit much on the phone. Their time together was a standing Monday morning breakfast time each week.

My greatest challenge in my son's adulthood was the transition from my role as a parent to my role as a friend. I had to learn to discipline myself to allow him his own decisions and not offer my advice unless he requested. He was very independent in his thinking and I understood that because I am also. I noticed that the more I stepped into my new role, the more I appreciated that he was an intelligent adult with a gift of spiritual wisdom.

Wes and I didn't always agree but we were still great friends and enjoyed sharing our lives with each other. We made precious memories together. In loss, accessing the good memories becomes a source of joy.

Precious Memories

Wes needed a haircut. He was three but almost four and big for his age. His slim body was topped with a full head of thick light brown hair. He eagerly climbed in the front seat of the car with me. I drove him to a local barber shop in a strip mall. He, just as eagerly, climbed up in the chair and the talking began. The barber was amused by what a sharp, talkative little kid he was.

Wes was used to adult conversation. He talked to me, his dad, his grandma and grandpa, his aunts and uncles and anyone else he could find to listen. He was well versed on many topics because he was nearly always with adults and was often included in their conversations. It seemed like the barber took advantage of the opportunity to see what all he could get out of the kid. It felt like an Art Linkletter moment where "kids say the darnedest things." The barber asked questions and Wes had all kinds of answers. The more he talked the more questions the barber had and Wes didn't disappoint as he divulged (slightly) embarrassing family secrets.

I was sitting and watching and listening with a bit of pride at my delightfully precocious child. I think everyone in the shop listened and enjoyed the show. When I got into the car with Wes, I pretended I was mildly upset with him, "Wes, why do you have to talk so much?" To which Wes earnestly replied without missing a beat, "But, Mama, it's my favorite thing!"

My Son, My Son

I never forgot that. I hadn't thought about talking in that way before but I had to agree that it was my favorite thing too. This moment in time from an ordinary day was sealed in my memory.

Wes was so much like me in temperament. He was his mother's child. I had a close relationship with him from the beginning. He was beautiful, fascinating, and a joy to be around. I began talking to him from the day he was born. We seemed to understand each other. When I observed him respond like me, whether good or bad, I'd say, "We're like two peas in a pod." As he grew up and into adulthood, he would say it back to me with his wry sense of humor. Sometimes it was a good thing but there were some habits and traits that we both wished I hadn't passed on. We shared those thoughts with a shared sense of humor. Of all the things we shared over the years, the most important ever was faith in Jesus.

Psalm 139

"Do you think that I'm not saved?" I was being counseled by a pastor and I wanted to clarify my salvation. He told me that he didn't know but I could make sure by praying . I knew the salvation prayer well. It didn't occur to me to pray with the pastor but I did pray when I got home. I also added an earnest prayer of surrender of my life to God. I call it my waving-the-white-flag-at-God moment. I made a firm commitment to go God's way and not my way any longer. This evening happened when Wes was nearly ten years old and our lives began to change.

One of the assignments the pastor gave me was to memorize part of Psalm 139. At first I thought he just meant to get really familiar with what it said but just in case he really meant memorize, I committed it to memory. I was in earnest to learn whatever I could about God's way and I repeated it to myself over and over. What I discovered was that God had made me the way He wanted me. That was earth shaking news to me because when I looked in the mirror I always felt that I wasn't quite good enough. As this good news seeped into my heart I realized that God had made Wes, not defective or flawed because of neurofibromatosis, but also the way He wanted him!

"For You created my inmost being; You knit me together in my mother's womb. I praise You because I am fearfully and wonderfully made; Your works are wonderful, I know that full well. My frame was not hidden from You when I was made in the secret place. When I was woven together in the depths of the earth, Your eyes saw my unformed body. All the days ordained for me were written in Your book before one of them came to be." Psalm 139: 13-16

The tears I often cried changed from hurt and pain to tears of joy! I was a changed woman. Wes watched it all happen in my life and it wasn't long before he believed and began to change also. I never doubted his salvation. His fervor might have gone up and down over the years ahead but not his deep-seated faith. It was always a comfort for me but that knowledge of his faith was critical on the day I was notified of his death.

The Call

I was at home cooking and working on an art project for a bible class I taught at a senior adult facility. I had taken a walk outside earlier in the day and it was a good day, a normal day.

I felt like I hadn't heard from Wes in a while. I guess I would describe it as an uneasiness. I remembered that I had called Wes the morning before which was unusual for me. Even though we were both morning people, I usually waited for him to call me in the evening. That morning I had a happy praise that I was bursting to share with him. I spoke a few brief minutes but he hadn't called me back in the evening. I had gotten him early before work and he sounded tired but he seemed his usual self, still full of wisdom and sharing my praise to God.

I tried his cell phone and my call was received because I heard faint voices in the distance but it just clicked off. I wondered if he was just someplace where he couldn't talk or had something happened? I lowered myself face down in the carpet to pray. My husband saw me and encouraged me to "wait to worry."

It was the afternoon of November 18, 2010.

Within a few minutes our phone rang. Caller ID showed my ex-husband's name. He never called me. I knew it couldn't be good. However, I braced myself for what any parent would dread, an accident or illness. In addition, I also knew his medical condition could cause troubling complications.

My Son, My Son

Wes' father's voice over the phone said, "Wesley is dead." I felt anger and wanted to argue. I thought if it was related to his condition there would be warnings. He didn't drive fast enough to be killed in a car wreck. They could do something. He hadn't been sick. Really, he was a remarkably healthy young man. Why would John say this? The rest of the conversation was a blur but I know it was short. The only thing I remember was that there was a gun.

There are no words for the feelings I had. I went back to my place on the floor. Not even tears would come until later. My husband came to comfort me. I was numb.

Survival skills I had learned since becoming a Christian had to be accessed. I had to think what I knew and believed about the great God who saved me and transformed me. God loves and works all things for good for those that are His. Wes was His, I was His. God has a plan and it's good. This was in some way part of His plan.

Sometime later, I was collapsed on the couch, the phone rang and I thought, "It's Wes, I've got to tell him of this awful thing that's happened." Then I realized how tragically wrong my thoughts were.

At some point, Wes' dad had to convince me that it wasn't an accident with a gun but that he had committed suicide. Those were words that would take me years to be able to say out loud. The long, dark journey of grieving and accepting the reality of my son's death by suicide began.

Shock set in. Questions came.

His Chair

Wes' dad and step mother opened the door for us. It was our first trip back to Wes' apartment. It was never again to be brightened by his presence. As Rob and I entered his living room I went to my favorite spot. There was my son's chair. It was a comfy recliner in front of the sliding glass door to the balcony. The view past the tree was a green space and empty parking lot and beyond there were views of beautiful sunsets. He was comfortable, even happy, in that one bedroom apartment. He loved to watch TV and that chair was his TV chair, his study chair, and his everything chair. My thoughts were racing. I was in shock. I was thinking "How did this happen?"

Beside his chair, was his open bible and his devotionals. Things were as they used to be but never would be again. The devotionals were <u>Our Daily Bread</u>, <u>Living Faith</u> and <u>Living Faith Kids</u>. They were still open to November 17. He had obviously read them on his last day. "I want these."

Things were not as they used to be. The place was cluttered and a new addition in his apartment was a kneeler. In those last months he had evidently wanted one at home. What was going on? What was troubling him that he had not shared?

I chose about ten other bibles Wes had in his apartment that he used. I couldn't take them all. He loved bibles and highlighters and had used them all. He liked gadgets and pens. He had highlighters in all colors and rulers to use to underline and note bible verses. He had journals full of notes he took. He was a serious student of the bible at home. There was no question about that as I looked around the room.

I wandered around the small apartment. My heart was crying, "Why?" I had to default to what I knew for sure:
- God has a plan.
- His plans are good.
- He knew the number of days of our lives before there was one of them.
- Some way this was an allowed part of the plan and He would work it for good.

I knew in my heart that I often wondered what complications from neurofibromatosis were ahead for Wes. Did God just spare him that? I had worried about complication from the time of his diagnosis in 1977. I learned very slowly over the years that my worry was unnecessary and useless. He had very few complications and even if he had more, my worry didn't change a thing. Now the irreversible has happened.

On the table beside his chair was a Thanksgiving card to send to someone. He was so thoughtful to remember older people who were lonely. He wasn't planning to be dead by Thanksgiving! My son, my son, what in the world had happened?

I remembered from Psalm 139 that God knows all our thoughts and the number of our days. He knew this. I was blindsided by this, He wasn't. God's plan is good. God will never leave me and He will help me. I couldn't see it but I had to take comfort in my faith. I can tell you faith works even when your heart is shattered and that is when you really need it!

The Grave

I have had enough medical procedures to know the blessed help an anesthetic is. God is our great Physician and I can only report that He applied anesthetic to my heart to help me through the first days and months of my grief.

Grief books talk about the fog. I was in the fog but I knew I had to keep one foot in front of the other and do what had to be done. My husband and I flew once again from Dallas to Kansas City but this time it was to bury my beloved child. Wes' father lived close to him and took over all the details.

I was no stranger to grief or funerals. My beloved mother had passed only fourteen months earlier. Her passing was something I had feared since I was a small child. She and I were very close and both Wes and I talked with her almost every day. As an adult I was given lots of time to see her decline and know she would go to be with Jesus and He would be here for me. I believed and experienced that peace. I had no such preparation for losing Wes.

No one who knew Wes well could believe this tragic news of suicide. Everyone was stunned. I was in a merciful shock. I'm not sure I could have been much help on the burial arrangements but I tried to respond when I was consulted. We would bury him in a graveside service on November 23. I had put in a call to our former pastor and friend. Both Wes and I had been close to him and his wife when Wes was a child. Yes, he would come to speak.
On that frigid, cloudy November morning Ralph and Linda Nite

showed up at the cemetery. Things had changed and I learned Wes' dad had consulted a priest to come and there was only going to be John and his wife and Rob and me. I called and left a message that the Nites didn't need to come. They didn't get the message and, as God would have it, they were there as a comfort and were able to say a few words about Wes. Ralph read some humorous quotes from Wes' Facebook posts that revealed his sense of humor. Then he shared the hope of scripture from I Peter about the salvation of our souls. It was a great comfort to me to have them there beside me.

Wes was buried near his apartment and his workplace on a peaceful hillside. It is a beautiful cemetery that he would have driven past nearly every day. The ground was frozen and covered in snow. I was frozen in survival mode.

His body was placed in the ground but not his spirit.

Let Wes Speak

I want you to know something about Wes' spirit. I want to allow you to hear him in his own words.

I would have had no interest in Facebook except that Wes loved it. He had amassed over seven hundred friends and was addicted to sharing his thoughts there. I now say praise God for Facebook!

With my husband's help we were able to print out some of the background information Wes had listed when he set his account up in 2009. It reflects both his humor and his faith. Please, laughter is expected.

> Under "Interested in":
> Women, Friendship, Dating.

> Under "Looking for"
> A relationship, Networking.

> Under "Likes and Interests" and "Activities:"
> God still performs miracles every day.

> If you want to burn our American flag, please wrap yourself up in it first.

> I'm proud to be a born again Christian, baptized and full of the Holy Ghost!

My Son, My Son

The happiest people don't have the best of everything, they just make the best of everything they have.

Dear Lord, please keep Your arm around my shoulder and Your hand over my mouth. Amen.

I am so good at cooking, even the smoke alarm is cheering me on.

I stop the microwave at 1 second to avoid the beeping.

Press like if Jesus is your Savior!!

When I die, I'll give my friends permission to change my status to "is chillin' with Jesus."

The older I get the less I care what other people think.

People see God every day, they just don't recognize Him.

I would rather walk with God in the dark than go alone in the light.

God understands our prayers even when we can't find the words to say them.

I hate it when I think of a really good comeback AFTER the argument.

I say "ouch" before I'm even sure it hurt…just in case.

I wish mosquitos sucked fat instead of blood.

If you think anyone who abuses an animal should be caged, press like.

When He was on the cross, I was on HIS mind!!!!

Let Wes Speak

I wish I was a better man. Every year, I realize how stupid I was the year before.

A happy relationship is made up of two good forgivers.

Oh, I'm sorry, I forgot I only exist to you when you need something.

If you think this country would be in better shape if we all started asking for God's help, press like.

I live for Christ. He is my way, my light, my strength, and my savior.

My Son, My Son

Making a Difference

I assumed the task of informing Facebook friends. What could I say?

I wrote:
To all John's friends on Facebook:
It is with great sadness I must report that my beloved son, John Wesley Czarnota, passed away on November 17, 2010. John's dad and I were in contact with him and had no reason to suspect anything amiss. He was happy at his job. We understand you all have questions as we do but we truly have no answers about the circumstances of his last moments. What we do know is that he had a strong faith that he shared openly. We deeply appreciate your condolences and thoughts about our son. He was a man who was kind and loving and will be greatly missed.

The following are a few of my favorite Facebook condolences:

My son listed a brother on profile. His name was Scott Czarnota. This was truly news to me so I contacted him directly after Wes' death.

> Scott Czarnota
> Hi Evelyn. My deepest sympathy to you in regards to John Wesley, we became friends on Facebook several years ago and became "Facebook brothers" because of our last name in

common…we communicated often on here because we were both very active, I looked forward to his daily posts and we often commented on each other's page…my mother, wife, and sisters were also friends of his on here and communicated with him too. Although we never met, I was very saddened to hear the news of his passing, and so was my family…thank you for contacting me and if there is anything I can say or do during this time to comfort you please let me know, I am a devoted Christian. John and I also had a very similar birthday in October. I am exactly 1 year and 1 day older than John was. I will truly miss my FB Brother. Sincerely, Scott Czarnota

Suzanne Czarnota
…I remember last Mother's Day, John wrote on my wall. Happy Mother's Day Mom. My thoughts and prayers go out to you and your family. I will definitely miss his posts. I live in NJ so I cannot attend his memorial service, but know that he is in Heaven with our Lord Jesus. Suzanne Czarnota (Scott's mom)

Joe Andrade
I was saddened to hear of John's passing. I also went to Miege with John and remember him always willing to help when a hand was needed.

Yolanda Vega
John as I sit here making your ribbons (FedEx tribute), I can't stop the tears. The gemstones I'm placing on them remind me of all the gems you will receive in heaven for all of the spiritual phrases you shared with us. You always reminded us to believe in our heavenly Father. I hope you know how inspirational they were. R.I.P., thanks for all the advice, you were so upbeat, I'll miss you. I know you're in a better place. I just wish it were here.

Julie Copenhaver
I taught John in '86-'87. He was always so full of interesting stories and details that he couldn't wait to share I reconnected with him on FB last year and I now will sadly miss reading his posts.

Making A Difference

Cassie Martin
You touched many lives and I will miss your posts—always so upbeat and looking at the glass half full rather than half empty!

Jo Waugh
You were so kind. Your love for God and your strong faith and belief are an inspiration to us all.

Jim Greer
He was one of my true friends. I did love him as a brother.

Nikki Bohn Tufte
John, you will be forever missed. You were always so good to my mother and me. A wonderful friend for the past 22 years. I don't know that I will ever meet another person with a kinder soul and more compassionate heart.

In preparing to write my son's story, I read his reflections from May 26, 2008 in his journal. He had written:

"When I stand before God to give my account what will I say? I hope it's I made a difference for the better."

I found the printed pages from Facebook that I'd saved. I reread them. Yes, my son, my son, you made a difference!

My Son, My Son

Sanctity of Life

I continued searching for clues in Facebook to see if my son had given any reason for his decision to end his life. My husband and I knew he didn't believe in suicide.

I found the following in his public Facebook posts just months before his death:

> May 22, 2010
> John Wesley Czarnota We should also pray that the life of every human person from conception to natural death might be enshrined and protected in our laws.
> May 27, 2010
> John Wesley Czarnota Never make a decision without stopping to consider the matter in the presence of God.
> May 30, 2010
> John Wesley Czarnota Let us pray that everyone will have an unfailing respect for all persons, from natural conception to natural death, for they have been created in the image of God.
> August 6, 2010
> John Wesley Czarnota
> Father God, I choose to speak blessing over my future. I choose to speak life over my future. Thank You for equipping me with everything I need to fulfill the destiny You have prepared for me. In Jesus' name. Amen.

I know these posts to be consistent with Wes' beliefs and values and the way he lived his life. He continued posting humorous thoughts and inspiration until his last day on earth. What in the world happened to change his mind? The only thing I could see from his posts was that the very last one was nonsensical. It confirmed what I believed. He was undoubtedly not thinking clearly. Why?

No Clues

"I want anything he wrote on." This was my request from Wes' dad. He collected and gave me a stack of notebooks and journals. I brought them home with me and went through them quickly to see if there were any clues as to his thoughts, intentions. I found nothing but his usual hopes and dreams and his strong faith.

Even though the sight of his handwriting was a stab of pain, I had push through my pain to read to get information. I had to know what he was thinking.

From his hand written journals, I found these treasures:

> August 1, 2010: Thank you for all "mothers" in my life. Mothers see things with different eyes—eyes that others miss. I couldn't begin to count the "moms" in my life.
>
> Granny, Ma, Donna---3 of the greatest women I know and I'm immeasurably blessed by them and for knowing them. I need to carry what they gave me and taught me and bless others with it!
>
> August 15, 2010
> Thoughts copied from a devotional book:
> Am I ready for eternity?
> Live in a way that death never finds you unprepared.
> When death comes it will find me in sanctifying grace.

My Son, My Son

From another book:
Believe without the slightest reservation.

Wes' last written journal stops nine weeks before his death.

September 13, 2010

Always keep a steady hope in achieving success.
1. examine life
2. face what needs to be done
3. pray for strength
4. Do it—determined to go on trying in spite of any failure which may occur.

From Ps. 96:2
Does my life, attitude, actions reflect "The Lord has saved us?"
Vs 21
Lord, help me to be the most generous I can be to others. Amen

Ps 96:2 CEV
Does my life, attitude, actions reflect "The Lord has saved us?
Vs 4
What is taking the place of God in my life?

Ps 37:3
We have a simple job to do, trust the Lord and live right.
We really don't have the time to focus on anyone else.
If my focus is on someone or something else, then I am not doing what God wants me to do.
Vs 4
What more than to please God should my heart want?
Vs 5 Why do I want the Lord to lead and seek His help when I'm in trouble or stressed, but not at other times?
Vs 9 Has my anger not caused me to sin?
Has my anger solved the problem?
Vs 18
What the Lord gives is eternal.

Vs19
Why is it that those who are the most generous, never seem to be in need?

Vs 21
Lord, help me to be the most generous I can be to others.
Amen

These words were comforting. They reflect my son's heart but added nothing to my search for "Why?"

My Son, My Son

Preparations

In the days after burying my beloved son, I was at home in Texas and just trying to breathe and do what had to be done. I had the TV on one afternoon but I wasn't really watching. My ears picked up and started listening to the ads that I usually tuned out. More ads for antidepressants and other medications were pitching to the afternoon crowd. I heard the reported side effects of thoughts of suicide and completed suicide. It dawned on me that this could be our answer.

Meanwhile, Wes' dad and stepmother were working at sifting through the contents of his apartment. I know it was an ordeal and one that I don't think I could have faced. What had happened to our beloved son? My once neatnik son had become messy and evidently stopped cleaning. He was a great cook and his cooking supplies were overflowing. Donna had found a mound of boxes of spices, many duplicates. He had been on a weight loss program along with several women from his work and there were all those supplies in abundance. The apartment was overflowing with stuff, recent purchases.

John combed through his financial paperwork. He found a receipt from a psychiatrist. He called the office and spoke with the doctor. She said she remembered Wes as being "so nice." She reported he'd expressed some anxiety and she'd prescribed a medication. Reportedly she said, "What are you doing here, most of my patients have problems!" When John asked the name of the drug, she declined and told him that she would need a subpoena to divulge that medical information. Neither of us knew anything about this.

My Son, My Son

My thoughts raced back to the time when I was in my forties and my hormones began to change and I experienced heart palpitations. I went to the doctor because I had never felt this before and I was sure something was wrong with my heart. Tests were run and the doctor told me I was depressed. I humorously say that I have a Ph. D. in depression because I have had much unwanted experience with it. I had learned over the years how to deal with it and what helped me. I knew I wasn't depressed. Things were better than they had ever been in my life. I tried to reason with the doctor but he prevailed with his diagnosis and urged me to take a medication, Zoloft.

I thought I'd give the doctor's advice a try to see if it helped. After all, he was the expert. I took the medication but nothing changed. I called the doctor and he increased the medication over the weeks ahead until I was at the maximum dosage. The subtle calm I'd felt at the beginning increased into what I would call a drug induced mania where I began a buying spree. I am a frugal person and didn't buy big ticket items but still I was spending. I remembered the time I had come home with a carload of purchases from a garage sale and another store where I bought damaged sale items. My phlegmatic husband's comment was "What are you going to do with that?"

Rob hardly ever makes a fuss over my spending but I began to look at the pile of junk and wondered myself. I reasoned that maybe I just wasn't thinking good. Then I thought about the medication that wasn't helping heart palpitations and decided to get off it. I did what, I would learn later, could be very dangerous and I quit cold turkey. My thinking returned to normal and I remembered what I knew and that was that I wasn't depressed! As I thought about the redundant supplies and impulse purchases in Wes' apartment, I was sure medication had to be a part of the puzzle.

Time was passing though and I needed to prepare for Wes' service.

Quotes

I decided to put some of Wes' favorite quotes together to be distributed at his upcoming memorial service. He would like that. He used Facebook to post quotes he found inspiring or humorous. We both loved well-crafted words. The apple doesn't fall far from the tree. He collected many books of quotations for reference.

I found the following jewels that truly reflected what he believed:

A man is no fool who gives what he cannot keep to gain what he cannot lose.
Missionary Jim Elliot on Salvation

Women and cats will do as they please, and men and dogs should relax and get used to the idea. Robert A. Heinlein

Bd. Teresa of Calcutta: God does not ask us to be successful; he asks us to be faithful.

Proclaim the gospel at all times; when necessary, use words. St. Francis of Assisi

Our souls are restless O Lord, until they rest in you. St. Thomas Aquinas

Make a gift of your life and lift all mankind by being kind, considerate, forgiving, and compassionate at all times….with everyone as well as yourself.

My Son, My Son

Dr. David Hawkins, Psychiatrist, physician, spiritual teacher

Our love for Christ is only as real as our love for our neighbor. Unknown

There is nothing small in the service of God. St. Francis of Sales

There is no depth to which we can fall that our Lord will not stoop to find us and reclaim us. Reverend Lloyd Ogilvie

A wise man will make haste to forgive, because he knows the true value of time. Samuel Johnson

Although the world is full of suffering, it is also full of the overcoming of it. Helen Keller

Contentment is the greatest wealth. Unknown

The center of God's will is our only safety. Betsie ten Boom

Let nothing disturb you
Let nothing frighten you
All things are passing
God alone does not change
Patience achieves everything
Whoever has God lacks nothing
God alone suffices.   St Teresa of Avila

The Photo

I needed to choose a photo for Wes' service to use on a memorial card with a bible verse (John 6:40) and his dates: Oct.17, 1973 to Nov. 17, 2010. My mind flashed back to a day in May, 2009.

It was a day Wes and I planned in advance. It was his day off and a day that I would fly to Kansas City to visit him and my mother. It turned out to be a beautiful sunny day. Wes was in good spirits when he picked me up at the airport. He had been exercising and had lost quite a bit of weight. I am a shopper and I always wanted to buy him clothes but he was a man and wasn't very interested. No, to be more correct, he was opposed to it. However, he needed a smaller size and he decided to indulge me this trip with the pleasure of shopping for clothes for him.

After we had shopped to the extent of his patience, we drove to visit Granny. Granny was eighty-seven and her health had been failing for quite some time. I knew the signs well since I had spent five years as a respiratory therapist in a hospital treating very sick and dying patients. There is a decline that doesn't reverse. I noticed the decline in Mama and knew our days with her were numbered. I lived in Dallas and Wes and Mama were in Kansas City. We not only talked every day but I also tried to go to visit frequently.

Mama had seven children and being a mother was her specialty, her calling. Wes was the firstborn grandchild and she babysat him for me often when he was a child. He became like her eighth child. They developed a close relationship that delighted me. She was looking forward to having both of us visit that day.

This day was a treat for all of us. Mama was up in her recliner in the living room when we arrived. I wanted Wes to show Granny his new clothes. He obliged me that and modeled a new shirt. I'd brought my camera and snapped a photo. He was sitting on an ottoman and looking at Granny and me. He was happy and grinning.

Later, when I discovered what a great photo it was, I sent it to him. Usually he didn't like his photos but even he liked this one. When he established a Facebook page, that photo was the one he used. His eyes sparkled as he was looking back at Granny and me with love.

I knew that was the photo I'd choose for the obituary and for his memorial service. I have to tell you though, for months after his funeral I couldn't even look at it. It was too painful of a reminder of my loss. God does heal though. Today it is a reminder of my gratitude for what I had—a beautiful son with love in his heart. I have the photo enlarged in a canvas print hanging in my home so I can look at it every day.

This precious photo was part of the outward preparations done for Wes' service, but I was trusting God for the preparation of my heart.

The Photo

My Son, My Son

The Timing

It was the evening before Wes' memorial service. Rob and I were making another heart wrenching trip to Wes' apartment. I looked around at the piles and piles of stuff. What could I take to remember my son and his spirit? I couldn't take much because I would have to take it on the airplane. Then I spotted a black leather bag in a collection of tote bags. I picked it up to see what it was and discovered it was a bag he took with him to work. I knew it was the last one he used because it had little packages of instant coffee in it that I had recently given him.

When we got back to our hotel suite I looked in the bag to see what all was in it. There was hand sanitizer, 2 small flashlights, small booklet, etc. I pulled the booklet out to see what it was. It was his calendar. Wes liked to keep order and track things. The booklet opened to September. There he had written Buspar with the Rx sign by it!

Rob was sitting on the sofa with the laptop open. I said, "Google this." I spelled the drug name and within seconds we were reading case study after case study of "completed suicide." The first one I read was a 34 year old man who committed suicide after being on the medication a short time. There was another piece of the puzzle confirming what I suspected.

My spirits lifted because I knew God had arranged these

circumstances so I didn't have to go to the service without knowing what had happened to my son. Praise God, Wes wrote everything down. Praise God, I picked up that bag. The timing of all that was a hug from God to me.

Did I sleep that night? I think so. The anesthetic for grief that God gave in the beginning allowed me long sleep.

The Service

The Service

The cold December morning came with sunshine. It was seventeen days after his death. Family and friends and church members arrived. My sister made a display of photos of Wes through the years. My niece brought flowers for the table displaying the memorial cards and sheets of quotes.

I stood along with Wes' dad to greet people arriving. Interestingly, the psychiatrist that prescribed the last medication for my son came. She introduced herself to me. In my fog of grief and without anger I said, "You're the one that prescribed the medication that killed my son." She responded, "But it was such a small dose…" I knew I wasn't capable of more discussion and I immediately took her and introduced her to his dad.

Wes' dad and I spoke in the service as well as two of his friends from work. The service was all beautiful but what I remember the most was what Wes' friend and supervisor said. I knew Carmen Johnson was an intelligent and well-educated single black woman in her fifties. She was no nonsense and had a very commanding presence. Wes loved her. He told me it took a while to get an understanding of her but once he did he felt like she was a good friend. She was also a committed Christian and they often shared their faith. Carmen's eulogy was a kind and generous declaration for his memorial.

Afterwards I asked Carmen to send me her notes and she sent me the following Facebook message entitled Eulogy.

"John was not only an employee, he was a friend. He was FedEx. He was never late, he had a 'can do' attitude, jumped to assist whenever or wherever he was needed.
If you knew John, John loved quotes and research. John would send uplifting, positive quotes to our team on a daily (basis). John was funny. He had some funny one liners that would keep you laughing all day.
As a friend, you could not have a better one. If you needed someone to listen to you, John was there. If you needed a helping hand, John was there. John's heart was huge. He remembered what you felt was important, your kids, your parents, your pets. He would ask you, "Do you need anything" or "Are you OK?" But most important John had a personal relationship with God. John was one of the most devout Christians I knew. He was not afraid to say he was a Christian. He had his bible and his prayer book always close to him. He wrote beautiful prayers. We had wonderful discussions and arguments that sometimes would arise, but as friends we would end those strong discussions agreeing to disagree, knowing we would revisit the same discussion later."

"To the family---this is my wish for you:
Comfort on difficult days,
Smiles when sadness intrudes,
Rainbows to follow the clouds,
Laughter to kiss your lips,
Sunsets to warm your heart,
Hugs when spirits sag,
Beauty for your eyes to see,
Friendships to brighten your being,
Faith so you can believe,
Confidence for when you doubt,
Courage to know yourself,
Patience to accept the truth,
Love to complete your life."

"It's not goodbye John, but so long, I know we will see you again."

The Service

I never for a second doubted that my son was in heaven. He believed and if he died he was with Christ. The service had that hope. With the help of God's anesthetic I made it through. Now the real work of accepting this reality started because I was stuck on earth without him.

The months ahead were filled with both grief and numbness. God was carrying me and I was hanging onto His promises.

My Son, My Son

A Poem

I don't know how long God's aesthetic lasted but it was gradually withdrawn to help me face my new life without my son. The first year I walked in the fog. I rested, read grief books, and put one foot in front of the other to get through daily life. No one can really tell you what it is like.

Wes' dad expressed his grief in a poem to publish in the newspaper on the first anniversary.

> The first year without you has been like one long winter's day.
> No sunny smile to let in beaming rays of light.
> No booming laughter to break up the clouds.
> No warming of the heart to cut the chill in the air.
> No words of wisdom to guide us through the fog.
> You are dearly missed by all who were blessed to know you.
> Your loving parents,
> John and Donna Czarnota
> Rob and Evelyn Hinds

The year anniversary was a milestone. It passed. Still, my presence dripped with grief. My heart still ached. I wondered how and when God would bring good out of this tragedy. Within a few weeks I would have a beginning of an idea of how God might work.

My Son, My Son

Comfort

You will find many others afflicted in the same way. I pondered that thought in my morning devotional time. It was January 11, 2012 and I was reading that day's devotion in <u>Streams in the Desert</u> by L. B. Cowman.

Comfort, comfort my people, says your God. (Isaiah 40:1)

"Store up comfort. This was the prophet Isaiah's mission. The world is full of hurting and comfortless hearts. But before you will be competent for this lofty ministry, you must be trained. And your training is extremely costly, for to make it complete, you too must endure the same afflictions that are wringing countless hearts of tears and blood. Consequently, your own life becomes the hospital ward where you are taught the divine art of comfort. You will be wounded so that in the binding up of your wounds by the Great Physician, you may learn how to render first aid to the wounded everywhere. Do you wonder why you are having to experience some great sorrow? Over the next ten years you will find many others afflicted in the same way. You will tell them how you suffered and were comforted. As the story unfolds, God will apply the anesthetic He once used on you to them. Then in the eager look followed

by the gleam of hope that chases the shadow of despair from the soul, you will know why you were afflicted. And you will bless God for the discipline that filled your life with such a treasure of experience and helpfulness."

"God comforts us not to make us comfortable but to make us comforters." John Henry Jowett

These thoughts swept over me and cheered me. The thought that I might use this tragedy to help others was just what I needed to rise up out of my grief. I couldn't wait to read it to my husband the next morning during our devotional time.

I read the devotional to Rob the next morning on January 12 as I'd planned and that very evening he called me from work and told me "awful news." I could tell from my husband's voice that he was stunned. His best friend and mentor had died instantly in a car crash earlier that afternoon. He was grieving a great loss to him.

As the devotional predicted, "You will find many other afflicted in the same way."

Days later as Rob and I stood by our friend's coffin, his wife began to ask questions. "Where is he and can he hear me?" Over the next months we were able to point her to scripture about what the bible says about faith and our destination when we die. We were able to pass on to a grieving widow the love and comfort we'd received from God.

God was using us. God was bringing good out of bad.

The Video

Within a few months, in June, 2012, I was visiting a chiropractor for health issues. I was the only patient waiting. I took the opportunity to poke around the room looking at the reading choices. On the receptionist's desk I saw a DVD with the title, <u>Dead Wrong: How psychiatric drugs are killing our children</u>. I commented, "My son is dead because of psychiatric drugs." The sweet young woman answered with heartfelt compassion, "I'm sorry for your loss." She then told me I could have the DVD.

I noticed later that the doctor had a stack of the DVDs to give out. The doctor provided what I believed God had arranged for me to see but I didn't know why. I brought it home thinking I might give it to Wes' grieving father. He was continuing to have Monday morning breakfast with Wes. Now it was at his grave. I thought maybe the DVD would comfort him.

It took me two weeks to gain the courage to watch the DVD myself. It was a documentary of one woman's story of the loss of her seventeen-year-old son interspersed with many other stories from bereaved mothers of younger children. Heartbreaking. It also contained interviews with medical professionals who recommended alternative treatment to anti-depressants. Testimony after testimony.

I called Wes' dad and told him the story from the video. The mother reported that her son had nightmares and some anxiety and she took him to a doctor who talked to them a few minutes and prescribed an anti-depressant. She asked about side effects and was told they were minimal. This was evidently before all the current warnings of suicide on the drugs' side effects. She learned later that anti-depressants can cause anxiety! She reported their tragic account of how her son was dead by suicide within nine weeks of getting the drug.

I knew Wes was only on the drug a few weeks also. Because the film brought up the issue, I had to face my avoidance of looking through his journals and calendar. I had stored them out of sight to ease the pain I felt when I looked at them. I retrieved the calendar and counted and it was almost identical to the story on the video.

A toxicology study given to us after Wes' death found that he was on four drugs all prescribed by doctors. The first three medications were evidently prescribed by his family physician. One was a muscle relaxer for low back pain that is also in the same class as anti-depressants. Another was the same anti-depressant I had taken in my forties, Zoloft. Another drug was for lowering his blood pressure. The fourth drug was the anti-depressant prescribed by the psychiatrist. Two of those drugs had interaction warnings that they should not have been taken together. Wes had lived for a while with the three drugs but was dead by suicide exactly eight weeks after adding the fourth medication.

This video was more evidence of the dangers of psychiatric drugs. Wes' dad didn't want to watch it. I could understand. But I had watched it and hoped God would use what I'd learned for good.

Sharing

"Have you told our class?" my friend asked. My husband and I had just shared the tragic details of my son's death with a new friend. She encouraged me to tell the bible class I taught at my church. She said, "It will help them." In my heart I knew it was a word from God for me. Wes had been gone nearly two years. I made notes and showed clips from the video about psychiatric drugs. I was able to make it through my talk but not without tears. While I can't measure how much it helped those that heard, I believe that it did and it sure helped me in my grief.

From that day forward I continued to say at least a few words about Wes' death whenever I had an audience. Every time people come up to share similar stories or tell me that they needed to hear it. After one of my performances as Corrie ten Boom, I said just a few sentences. A young teenager came up and thanked me and quickly left. Afterwards, the meeting director told me that she was a visitor to the church and had been put on anti-depressants because her parents were being divorced. In my opinion it would be normal to be depressed in that situation but not necessarily reason to medicate a young mind. I thought that it could be possible that hearing my story saved her life.

My story is certainly not the one I would have chosen. Still, it's the one God has allowed. I want to be faithful to share what I've experienced through this journey. I know the written word can go where I can't go and that the day would come when it was time to write. It would be the next step in God bringing good out of bad.

Treasures

Two more years passed.

I had stored the treasures that I had taken from Wes' apartment. The collection of bibles, spiral notebooks, note cards, and a calendar were better than gold to me. However, in the first months, just the sight of his handwriting would bring up fresh grieving on top of the heaviness I was trying to wade through. I realized I had to put them away out of sight. I stored them in a chest until I could heal a little.

I remembered the first Mother's day after his passing. I pulled them out to remember him. It began a crying episode that would leave me with still swollen eyes and a headache the next day. For my emotionally shattered health, I put them away again.

Whenever I thought about those treasures, it would bring up the memories of my grief and not of my son. They were both precious but also painful. I left them for nearly four years before I could face them. To begin my writing project, I started by bringing it all out in the open and put the stacks of journals and papers on our dining room table. I wanted easy access for my writing.

One morning I was sorting and pulled out one notebook that was a columnar accounting book. I remember seeing it and thinking about how hard he was working on keeping his finances in order. I think maybe he had listened to Dave Ramsey and this ledger had every little

expense neatly recorded. There was a father's day gift for Rob. There were Starbuck's charges. He loved to take his friend Carmen her favorite Starbucks coffee drink. I remembered reading the prayer he had recorded that he wanted to be generous.
Inside this account ledger were papers I had not seen before or maybe they just had not registered in my state of grief. They were medical lab reports. John Wesley Czarnota, 10-17-73, and date of test, 5-24-10. His blood work stats were recorded and the doctor had scribbled, "good labs" at the bottom of the paper. My heart was stabbed once again. The evidence that he was in good medical health five months before his death is clear. But part of my heart still ached.

I heard a preacher say once, "If you want to see a person's priorities, look at their checkbook." I was looking at Wes' checkbook in this ledger. For my birthday gift he had written—Ma. I saw entries for Donna. She was a good and loving stepmother to my son. She was an experienced mother when she married Wes' dad and came to love Wes too. She was his ally in conflicts with his dad and he appreciated her.

There was another entry for Maria. I'd never met her but I talked to her on the phone after his death. Maria was the mother of Crystal. Crystal was Wes' internet friend. They enjoyed their online relationship and often watched movies together. They both loved pets and she probably enjoyed laughs as Wes did. I remember when Wes called me on December 24, 2006. He was annoyed. When he had talked with Crystal earlier, she said she would call him back but she hadn't. The next day he called and told me that he'd learned that Crystal had died. She had a seizure disorder that had suddenly taken her life. I could tell by his voice he was stunned. That was what I personally know about now…the shock of grief.

Wes continued to honor Crystal's memory at his church and sending cards to her Mom. He kept in touch with her on the phone. She sent him Crystal's bible. In a journal I came upon this prayer he wrote on August 5, 2007.

Treasures

> Father God of mercies,
> Comfort Maria and revive her drooping spirit. If possible in Your Holy will send Crystal to her in some way to help her move on. Show me a way I can be a comfort to her. Help her to realize she needs the church and bring her to one that will love her and welcome her with open arms to minister to her. May she start reading the book (Purpose Driven Life) and find the comfort in it that I did. Keep her family close to You so they can help her. Don't let anyone, most especially those with good intentions, including me, say anything remotely hurtful. Don't allow her to look down on herself. Cause her to go to You in prayer and to Your word as often as necessary. Thank you Lord for listening and for working. Amen

I drew comfort from reading his prayer for this bereaved mother that he never met. I believed this was a prayer he would have had for me. He would want me to be able to move on with my life.

These written treasures reveal my son. His kindness. His generosity. I was amazed at how I was being comforted by reading his words, seeing his priorities in his accounting. He is not here but how thankful I am for who he was! That was my silver lining in the work of writing.

I began my writing with the hope God will continue to use me and bring good out of bad.

My Son, My Son

Gold

I was racking my brain for where I might have stored other papers that I knew I kept somewhere. We moved a year ago and I still have not completely located everything, especially storage items. Anything could have happened to them. I was on the search because they would help me in writing about Wes.

As my last ditch effort I unloaded the top of the cedar chest to check what was in it. Wes' baby cup and spoon. A red corduroy robe I made for him when he was about four. Other keepsakes and a plastic storage bag of paper items. Gold!!!

I share my treasures with you that you might know more about my son's spirit and be encouraged.

Wes had emailed me a copy of a letter he had sent to my mother probably in her birthday card in July of 2003.
"Dear Granny,
I have had the honor and pleasure of being your grandson for almost 30 years. I also take great pleasure of being the first grandchild. I know you love all of us grandkids the same, but I feel that you have loved me longer. I will never forget the time one very cold winter when Grandpa brought home this newborn calf and put it in a big box by the refrigerator to keep it warm. Well, the next morning I got up first and it was very early and went in to see about it and I was petting it and just decided to

get into the box with it. I was lying next to the calf when you came in to see about me and asked if it was dead, I said, "No, Grandma if it were dead I wouldn't be in the box with it."

It's great to be able to call you every day and visit you every week. Not many have that luxury or privilege. I treasure every moment I spend with you and every conversation we have had. I know I enjoy our daily phone calls and our Sunday lunches and conversations in the living room.

I owe a lot to you Granny and I don't say I love you enough. A lot of who I am can be credited to you. You helped raise me and are still raising me. Not to mention you are still raising all of us. You've done a good job, maybe too good because we are still hovering around you and needing you.

The picture of you with butter on is one of my favorites. (When he was two or three years old, Wes told Grandma to wear butter. She couldn't understand what he meant so he took her to her closet and showed her a dress. She explained that she had said, "I need to put on a better dress." He confused better with butter and it was a humorous story that they loved to share.") You have been wearing butter for years and you get better and better every day.

With all my love,
Wesley"

I also found a paper with a poem for me from 05-10-2008

Mom,
I have never written a poem before, but this came to me today. I know it's kind of simple, but that is part of the beauty of it. I hope you like it.

E is for EVERYTHING because that is what you give in your work and ministry and what you have taught me to give.
V is for VICTOR and Corrie's message is Jesus is Victor.
E is EASE because your presence puts people at ease.
L is for LOYALTY and that is the example you are and give to your family and friends.
Y is for YEAST and you are God's yeast.

N is for NOBILITY for like Esther, Ruth and the Proverbs 31 woman, you are a woman of nobility and I am proud to have you as my mother.

Wes

I found these emails entitled "sermons." They were sent out to a list of friends and family long before Facebook.

Thursday, July 4, 2002 8:07am
Good Morning,
Happy Independence day to you. I hope you have a great day today in whatever you do. I plan on being lazy today. There is a Law and Order marathon on A&E, so I will watch some of that. I will also spend the day remembering those that brought this freedom to me. First to our Lord Jesus Christ who brought freedom from the Law and sin; who gave His life and rose from the dead to give me eternal life. But I don't want to forget those men and women who gave so I could live in a land of political and religious freedom. Those people had a belief and bravery to do what it takes to get the job done. I don't want to let the memory of what they have done be in vain. Today we still have to fight for freedom. We still have the job to do of taking the Gospel to as many as possible. Everyone that we come into contact with is an opportunity to show them Jesus. I commit myself right here and now to do this. I just wanted to share this with you. I hope this may inspire you to do what you think God is leading you to do. Take care and have a safe day.
In Christ's love and mine,
John
If you get the chance today, listen to James Dobson of Focus on the Family radio program. They are playing Adventures in Odyssey's show today from Paul Revere's ride. It is so good. I have heard that program several times and it always brings tears to my eye. In fact hearing that prompted me to write this.

Saturday, February 1, 2003 9:17 PM
Hello,
As I sit here tonight thinking about the day's events and praying for the families of those onboard the Columbia, I am reminded

My Son, My Son

of the Challenger that happened some 17 years ago. I remember being in 6th grade at the time and our teacher Mrs. Chin telling us about it. I was in Catholic school then and we did not even stop to pray for anyone. I know my relationship with the Lord was not as close as it is now (and it still needs to be closer than it already is) I think I remember saying some sort of prayer. But all thru the day when I heard the news or thought of the events I was in prayer for the families and those involved. I am so glad we have a believing President. The news said that after he spoke to the families of the astronauts he went in to his private study. While it is not known what went on there, I believe he was praying to our Lord and Savior Jesus Christ. Now as much as always we need to pray for President Bush. I am ashamed to say I don't pray for him as often as I should; you can bet that I will be praying for him more often. Not only for him but for all our leaders. I think we sin when we don't pray for our leaders. (prayer will be a later sermon)

What inspired me to write this other than the leading of the Holy Spirit is hearing about the men and women onboard Columbia. It's amazing the country we live in and the variety of people that make up our fine country. We had an American, an Israeli, and an Indian (she was from India.) What inspired me most is to hear about the lives of these brave souls. Everyone onboard knew the risks they were taking and still went on anyway. They were all professional and passionate in their fields. What also got me was that I need to make goals and work toward them and not let anything get in the way of those goals (of course those goals need to be given by the Lord and committed to Him in prayer and to keep praying over those goals until they are completed and then to make more goals) and that is what these people did. They also had a variety of experiences that they brought to the group and that is exactly like the Kingdom of God. We are all different and we all can bring something valuable to the world when we work together. As I grow in the Faith I believe God did not intend for us to be loners or hermits. Mom, that last part was for you. I am tired of trying it alone because alone does not work. The work they had to do to prepare for this was not an easy task I am sure. I am

Gold

ashamed to say that I have taken the easy way out of things because I was too lazy to put the work involved to achieve things. While these people were not young and not old either, they were older than most of us reading this. I often wonder what God is leading me and you to do later in life and what we are to learn on the way there. I want to learn as much as I can so I can do more for Him as He call calls me to act. God brings us to things when we are ready for them and the more ready we can be, the more we can do for Him. The crew was doing something they loved and worked for. I think we all need to find out what we are passionate about and love to do and commit to God and jump in and do it. I know that is going to be my prayer, for the Lord to show me what I need to be passionate about and how to achieve it. I will pray that for you as well. (Sorry that might have been a lot for one paragraph, but the intent is not necessarily proper writing skills here but on of touching people for Him.)
I am also reminded that God is still God and He is still in control. While we don't know and may not ever know this side of heaven why He let this happen, He is still God. While this can't even begin to compare to 9/11, it's still another chance for believers to be sharing Him and bring Him to the world. "Let your light shine before men, that they may see your good deeds and praise your Father in Heaven." Matt. 5:16 I wonder how many Christians are being a light today and what kind of light are we being. I am tired of being a dim light. We have the light of the world in us and we ought to shine so bright, brighter than the brightest halogen lamp there is (this is for you technical people out there.) (Hey, who said sermons can't have humor in there and something for everyone.) The only way we can be sure to shine brightly is to keep in prayer, bible study, and be filled with the Holy Spirit each day. When we fail to do that our light won't shine as it should. Ann Graham Lotz said that "Having your devotions at the end of the day is like tuning your instrument after the symphony." I would encourage you to have at least some sort of devotion when you start your day. While we all have times of the day that are better than others to get with God, we can at least give Him something at the start of the day, seeing that He is the one that gave us another day.
Well, this is all I will say for now. I hope I made some sense

here. I know I am first preaching this to myself.
In His grip,
John

"Nobody ever outgrows Scripture, the book widens and deepens with our years." Charles Spurgeon

February 3, 2003
What shall we say then? Shall we go on sinning so that grace may increase? By no means! We died to sin; how can we live in it any longer? Romans 6: 1-2
These verses have always struck me as difficult, not to understand but follow. It wasn't until I started to look deeper into my heart and asked the Holy Spirit's guidance did I begain to grasp this a little better. I don't think we will ever be able to fully grasp this verse this side of heaven though.
I see here that we have a choice of whether we listen to the sin nature that is in us or not. I do know that where the mind goes the body will follow, so if we fill our minds with the things of Christ how can we sin? Watchman Nee said, "Since I am crucified with Thee from sin and self I am set free, how can I still enjoy the world or seek its vanities unfurled?" I ran across this quote in a book on Christian quotes and it reminded me that we have a choice of Who we listen to. Since we are Christians why would we listen to anyone other than our Lord and Savior Jesus Christ. Why would we listen to anyone other than the one who bought us with His life? Do we want to listen to the father of lies? If we are thinking only about ourselves maybe we do, but that is so WRONG and not to mention sad. I have found it tiring to live in sin any more. There is nothing fulfilling or good or joyful about a life of sin and defeat. This verse means freedom. We don't have to live that way. After all Christ gave you the way out. (That's a portion of another verse that you will just have to look up for yourselves.) There is a lot more to this verse other than what I have said, but I think this gets the jest of it and skims the top for us to understand. There is also the point that we hurt Jesus and our relationship with Him when we sin. Sure we will never be free of sin this side of heaven and sure He

has forgiven us our sins past and present. But why would we choose to do what we know will hurt someone? We don't do this to our friends and family, why do it to our Lord! I have been praying for the Lord to keep me from sin and that requires the Lord and for us to be alert. Every time I fall into sin it's usually because I was not watching and certainly not praying. Christ and the Devil can't dwell in the same place.

Pray for me that I will be watching and praying. I will be praying for you.

John

February 4, 2003

I did not get a chance to see much of the memorial service for Columbia. What I did get to see was the last 5 minutes of the service. The ending prayer was really good and it was said by a Navy Chaplain. That however is not what I wanted to talk about. I saw our President and his wife in the crowd. As they left at the end of the service, they walked out first and they were arm in arm and then they were holding hands. It seems when you see them together they are always holding hands. To me that is very refreshing to see and to know that he is a family man, a committed Christian, and a man who loves his wife. After our last President (sorry to those who liked him, there are many of you) it's a wonderful change. I think seeing Bush and what he stands for, his morals are what the country was founded on and what the forefathers intended. This is not what the sermon is about either, but something I thought should be said.

As I caught the tail end of the memorial service today they played, "It is Well with my Soul." I always liked this song, but the words really hit me today and I hope they will hit you too. I will tell you what they say to me and hope you will agree.

Chorus

It is well with my soul, it is well, it is well, with my soul.

To me this is saying no matter what happens our soul can be at rest. We serve the Creator of the world and everything that happens has gone through His hand first. Why would things not be well when screened by God? This also reminds me of a quote by Charles Spurgeon, "Anxiety does not empty tomorrow of its sorrows but only empties today of its strength." Why should we worry about things we have no control over?

Verse 1

When peace like a river attendeth my way, When sorrows like sea billows roll, Whatever my lot, Thou has taught me to say, It is well, it is well with my soul.

Interesting words if you read them carefully and ponder what they say. How peaceful is a river? Depending on the river, it can go either way, but what I see here is an image of the quietest field in a snow capped mountain with the green of the grass and gentle flowing river running over smooth rock that the water has worn over through time. The day could be a warm but not hot Spring day or one of the last nice days of Fall. However you see it, it's a calming influence on whatever has recently happened.

When sorrow like sea billows roll.

I know nothing about the writer of this hymn, but this might lead me to believe he has some sort of sea background. I am reminded of the time when the Disciples are out in the boat on the sea and a storm is raging and along comes Jesus walking on the water. The storm has to be fierce almost like a hurricane maybe. Life's storms can seem so fierce. But we can stand firm in the midst of the storm because we know Who is holding our hand in the midst of them. "Who am I that even the winds obey Him." Keep this in mind the next time sorrow comes your way, or for that matter what seems like a hurricane.

Verse 2

Though Satan should buffet, though trials should come, Let this blest assurance control, That Christ hath regarded my helpless estate and hath shed His own blood for my soul.

(Buffet a blow: without hand or fist, a violent shock or concussion to strike as with the hand or fist, to strike against or push repeatedly, to contend against battle, to force one's way.) Sounds just like the works of the devil and contrary to the way of Christ. Isn't it interesting that Christ will never force His way on us, but it seems like that's all the Devil does. These are strong and nasty words if you think about them and there is no fun whatsoever in them, but regardless we can still be at peace when we know the God of Peace.

Blest assurance control.

Gold

That is assurance that you can't doubt. Kind of a no brainer.
That Christ hath regarded my helpless estate.
We have nothing to offer God and nothing we can do to save ourselves. It's all grace. We serve a gracious God. We don't deserve a thing but death and life away from God.
But He had a better plan.
And hath shed His own blood for my soul.
Let's see, another no brainer. See John 3:16 I won't even go on.
Verse 3
My sin O the bliss of this glorious thought, My sin, not in part, but the whole, Is nailed to the cross, and I bear it no more:
Praise the Lord, praise the Lord, O my soul.
Wow, there is a lot here. Not only did He take away our past sins but every future sin we will ever commit. He died once for all, the just for the unjust (can you find out the verse that this is a part of, I love to see if you can find it, let me know when you do). How freeing this is to be free of sin once and for all. (You might want to remember my last sermon.) After all this how can you not praise Him!
Verse 4
And, Lord, haste the day when my faith shall be sight, The clouds be rolled back as the scroll: The trump shall resound and the Lord shall descend, Even so it is well with my soul.
And Lord, haste the day when my faith shall be sight.
That sounds like when we get to heaven. We will see Him face to face. What a great day that will be. If you are ready to meet Him, you should want that day to be soon. "Now there is in store for me, the crown of righteousness which the Lord, the righteous judge, will award to me on that day—and not only me, but also to all who have longed for His appearing" Timothy 4:8 I think this is what the writer of this hymn had in mind on this verse.
The clouds be rolled back as a scroll.
If you have ever seen a scroll, especially the kind used in biblical times, this will be a good image. I can just see the clouds parting right now. Can't you? It will be like nothing we have ever seen before. If you look at the sky as the sun comes out and after a rain you can get a picture of this. Maybe not the best picture, but a picture nonetheless.

My Son, My Son

The trump shall resound and the Lord shall descend.
I think this is the trump of the second coming or maybe even the rapture. Whatever you hold to, be it pre-trib, mid-trib, or post-trib, you know that the trump will sound and the Lord will descend. I think it will be a trumpet everyone can hear. We don't think about trumpets all that much today, but in Bible times trumpets were used a lot. You heard them to send warning and you heard them for celebrations. For believers this trump will be for celebration; like none the world has ever seen.
So it is well with my soul. There is a lot that I have said here and a lot more to be said here. I hope this makes you think the next time you sing this hymn. I think it was fitting that they played this for the memorial for Columbia.
Hymns are a great thing. I encourage you to get a hymnal and read through a hymn a day. Read the words. Think about what they mean. Think about what the writer wanted to convey when it was written. When we sing them at church they do go fast and you can't always think about what you are singing. I hope you will the next time. You may realize how they are used to praise God and teach us again and again about Him.
Your brother in Him,
John

February 7, 2003
Have Thine Own Way, Lord!
This hymn really hit me hard. I was just looking thru this old hymnal and ran across this and thought it would make a good sermon.
1.   Have Thine own way Lord! Have Thine own way! Thou art the Potter, I am the clay: Mold me and make me after Thy will, while I am waiting, yielded and still.
Do we really want God to have His own way? I am ashamed to admit I tend to want my way. This way is definitely better, but I often forget that. But then I am reminded of Jer. 29:11. (Look it up.)
Thou art the Potter I am the clay; Mold me and make me after Thy will, while I am waiting, yielded and still.
If you know anything about pottery you will really appreciate

this. While I don't know a lot about it, I have a general idea. The potter does the work of molding and shaping to the form of his or her choice and the clay obeys because it's in the potter's hands. What a good description this is of Christ. He has the omniscience! He is the One to be in control. Our job is to do what He says. Just look up Is. 29:16. We need to be quiet and still in His hands while He works on us. I could go on here, but I think you get the idea.

2. Have Thine own way, Lord! Search me and try me, Master today! Whiter than snow, Lord wash me just now, as in Thy presence humbly I bow.

Search—to look through (a place, area, etc.) carefully in order to find something missing or lost, to examine (a person, object, etc.) carefully in order to find something concealed, to explore or examine in order to discover, to examine properly, to look into or question or scrutinize, to pierce or penetrate, to uncover or find by examination or exploration.

The list can go one, I never thought of it in exactly this way before. God has done all this from the beginning. See Ps. 139. Again I can go one, but I think this already speaks volumes.

Whiter than snow, Lord wash me just now, As in Thy presence humbly I bow.

I see Ps. 51:7 here.

as in Thy presence humbly I bow

When we are in His presence we will bow. I see Phil. 2:10 here. We can bow now by choice or when He comes to judge the earth.

3. Have Thine own way, Lord! Wounded and weary, help me I pray! Power all power, surely is Thine! Touch me and heal me, Savior divine!

(Wounded-adj.-physically or mentally exhausted, fatigued, tired, characterized by or causing fatigue, impairment or dissatisfied with something.)

While this can describe what others can do to us, we can do to others, what our sin does to God, what our sin does to us, and the list can go on.

Power, all power, sincerely is Thine! Touch me and heal me, Savior divine!

Only God is powerful. Only He has the power to heal. The

scripture references for this are numerous.
4. Have Thine own Way, Lord! Hold o'er my being absolute sway! Fill with Thy Spirit till all shall see Christ only, always, living in me.

Absolute-adj., being fully or perfectly as indicated, complete, perfect, free from restriction or limitation or exception, outright unqualified, positive or certain or definite.

The list can go on, but you get the general idea. This describes the Lord.

(Sway-verb-to move or swing to and fro as something fastened at one end, to move or incline to one side, to incline in opinion or sympathy, to fluctuate as in opinion, to wield power or execute rule.)

You can see a lot here too. I can see us both before and after we become Christians here. Before Christ we were our own, doing our own thing our own way. After Christ, we sway with Him. This might not be the best reasoning, but it is all I've got for right now.

Fill with Thy Spirit till all shall see Christ only, always, living in me.

While we will never be perfect this side of heaven, we can be and should pray to be filled daily with His Spirit. When we are filled with His Spirit we will exhibit the fruits of the Spirit: peace, love, joy, goodness, kindness, gentleness, faithfulness, self-control, and last but certainly not the least one, the one I always seem to forget…patience. Without His Spirit we don't truly have any of these, but with Him we can and should have all of these.

I hope I made sense here. This came together pretty quickly and I know there are things that I missed. But for a first real read thru of this hymn, this is what I got. I hope you will prayerfully read thru this too. Do tell me if I forget anything and/or, by all means, add something to it.

Yours in Christ,
John

February 13, 2003
Delight yourself in the lord and He will give you the desires of your heart. Ps. 37: 4

Gold

(Delight Noun 1. A high degree of pleasure or enjoyment; joy; rapture 2. Soothing that gives great pleasure.
Verb 1. to give delight to 2. To have or to take pleasure)
I have to admit this verse confused me the first few times I read it. I thought knowing me, my heart would desire the wrong thing. Too often what I would want for me may not necessarily be what the Lord wants for me. I even went so far as to pray "Lord, give me what Your heart wants not mine; because I will ask You for the wrong thing."
I guess I prayed that for a while before I realized (with the help of the Holy Spirit by the way) that if I delight the Lord, which I take to be doing what He wants, I will want what He wants for me.
The New Living Bible says, "Take delight in the Lord" I like the word take here because to me it is saying to catch or to get. If you get what the Lord says you will ask for what the Lord wants. I checked 8 different translations and all of them say this in almost exactly the same way. The best might be the Contemporary English Version that says, "Do what the Lord wants, and He will give you your heart's desire."
What amazed me most was all of the translations used the qualifier "the Lord." Those are two of the most important words in the whole verse. The Lord is the One who is important. He is or at least should be our everything. He is the reason why we are here and the One who we are here through. (see Ps. 139:13)
In order for God to give us our heart's desires we do need to be in prayer and Bible study. It is only there that we will know what He desires and expects of us. For Him to give us what we want we need to be doing what He wants.
1 John 5:14 says, "This is the confidence we have in approaching God: that if we ask anything according to His will, He hears us."
I hope your desire will be the Lord's desires. You know how to find out His desires.
Father God, thank you for giving us your Son. Thank you that by His death and resurrection we now have fellowship with you. Thank you, that your desire was never to lose fellowship with us. It was our sin that broke that fellowship. Thank you that it was Your desire to send us Jesus to bring that fellowship back.
Thank You that You gave us Your word and the Holy Spirit so

we may know what Your desire is. I pray that we will grow closer and closer and Your desire will be our only desire. Thank You that You will give us our desires. In Jesus name, amen.
Your brother in Him,
John

March 10, 2003
Sometime back I sent you an email on the memorial service for Columbia. In that letter I was telling you about President Bush handing his handkerchief to the mother of a small boy sitting next to him and then after the boy was done with it he gave it back to his mom and she handed it back to the President and He put it away. Well, as it turns out that boy was the son of Mission Commander Rick Husband.

I found this out a few weeks ago when I saw People magazine and it had pictures and profiles of each of the crew and their families. What I did not know until watching Zola Levitt this morning was that Rick was a Christian.

Rick's life verse was Proverbs 3:5-6. "Trust in the Lord with all your heart and lean not on your own understanding; and in all your ways acknowledge him, and he will make your paths straight." This I am sure is the life verse of many people. I know it has been one of my favorite verses. I will not write a sermon on this verse right now, but may decide to do one later. What little I will say about this verse is that we are nothing aside from the Lord and it is not about us, it is about God.

Rick was a committed Christian and lover of the Jewish people. He was excited about having the first Israeli on board the flight. He was also a man of prayer. In fact his prayer partner was Mike Anderson, the African American on board.

Rick was also a committed husband and father who believed strongly in family devotions. He went as far as to video tape devotions for his children. One for each of the days that he was gone. I don't know about you but that is what I call commitment. Those videos will be a lifetime treasure for those kids. It should also be a lesson to all of us. Not only that family devotions are important, but should not be missed when one is out of town or in Rick's case, out in space.

Zola Levitt said that he was asked to give a benediction for the crew before the launch and he said he was having difficulty finding a verse for it. Well, the Lord gave him Numbers 6:24-25: "I pray the Lord will bless and protect you and that He will show you mercy and kindness. May the Lord be good to you and give you peace." I ran across this verse some 6 to 8 months ago and I have it posted on my desk at work and I try and pray it daily for my friends and family. I pray it daily for all of you also. I see it a fitting prayer for any occasion.
Your brother in Him,
John

My Son, My Son

Dr. Breggin

Shortly after Wes' passing in 2010 my husband had looked through the internet and found a video of a psychiatrist testifying before Congress on the subject of suicide among soldiers. He reported that the ones committing suicide were mostly not those who had been in combat. Dr. Breggin testified that the new generation of psychotropic drugs were extremely dangerous and they are being given to heavily armed young men! It was more evidence of what had happened to Wes. I remembered being impressed by this psychiatrist's bravery to blow the whistle on the drug manufacturers.

Recently, my friend Patty Raulston emailed a video link she found on the internet featuring that same doctor speaking in several videos about helping disturbed and suicidal patients. Patty is a nurse and is currently working in a hospital with patients who have attempted suicide. She sees firsthand how medication can easily be part of the tragedy of suicide. The videos were a series entitled "Simple Truths." They are available through the website www.Breggin.com or on You Tube.

I was intrigued to know more about Dr. Breggin's work. I went to the website and ordered more information. <u>Medication Madness: The Role of Psychiatric Drugs in Cases of Violence, Suicide, and Crime</u>, <u>Toxic Psychiatry</u>, <u>The Anti-Depressant Fact Book</u>, <u>Your Drug May be Your Problem</u>. These books were helpful in giving more confirmation about the dangers of these drugs. They also confirmed what Rob and I suspected about the suicides and shootings we hear

regularly about on the news. We now look around and can clearly see the lives and reputations ruined by anti-depressants.
The books also supported what I learned in the video I'd watched in 2012, the "chemical imbalance" label is only a theory and not supported by facts. I guess the most alarming new thing I learned is that long term use of anti-depressants can cause brain damage!

While I was on the website I also ordered <u>The Heart of Being Helpful: Empathy and the Creation of a Healing Presence</u> and a DVD series on <u>Empathic Therapy</u>. The whole idea of empathy and a healing presence rang true with my Christian beliefs to fulfill Jesus' command to love one another. Both of the materials taught me new ways of thinking about myself and my experiences as well as helping others. Being helpful is what all Christians are called to do! The foremost takeaway for me from the therapy videos was that the patient is removed from the victim role and given empowerment. Dr. Breggin kindly counsels, "Troubles are generally meant to be dealt with by human beings." The therapist helps the patient in finding constructive ways to deal with their problems instead of chemically altering the patient's brain with medication.

Two months later, September 14, 2014, I had a "chance" meeting in person with Dr. Breggin at the Denver airport. I was waiting for a flight and mindlessly people watching. A man was getting onto an escalator just a few yards from me. He was on the going down side and I was looking mostly at the side of his face. I quickly exclaimed to Rob, "That's Dr. Breggin!" Rob had watched the videos with me twice and agreed it had to be him. I hopped up and rushed to go after him. I went quickly down the steps and caught up with him. He was very weary after two flights and was a bit surprised. I quickly told him we had watched his videos several times and how his research and findings help confirm what I suspected about the drugs and my son's suicide. I think I just babbled as fast as I could because he had another flight to catch.

I fished a card out of my overstuffed purse and gave it to him. It was my card for my Corrie ten Boom portrayal and I briefly explained that. I knew from his writings that he was Jewish and had an interest in the Holocaust. I told him I wanted to write to him. I knew I hadn't really communicated well my appreciation of his work and I wanted to write to make it clearer.

Back at home I began rereading The Heart of Being Helpful. I believed Wes would have benefitted from Empathic therapy. Anybody would. Talking helps. A loving presence helps. I am so grateful for Dr. Breggin and his life's work.

My takeaways from what I've learned from Dr. Breggin, the bible, other sources boils down to:
- Depression is real.
- Depression needs to be addressed.
- Medication is not the answer.
- People need to talk.
- Help is available.
- Love is the heart of being helpful.

My Son, My Son

Gratitude

In the process of writing this book, a timely email arrived in my inbox from www.breakfastwithFred.com. Fred is Fred Smith. For several years before Fred's passing my husband and I were privileged to sit under his teaching on Saturday mornings. Fred was a wise man and mentored many people, including Zig Ziglar. After his death Fred's daughter founded a ministry that dispenses his wisdom from his writing and speaking career. Fred continues to mentor! This writing rang true of the Fred we knew and what I've learned about depression.

"Down, but not Out" by Fred Smith

"Research shows a young man today is ten times more likely to be depressed than his father, and twenty times more than his grandfather. The artificial measures we put on our lives contribute greatly to this condition. Our faulty, "have it all" definition of success creates an atmosphere ripe for depression. Our generation of materialism leads to degeneration.
The greatest defense against depression is gratitude - or so I have found. I once spoke to an audience with a severely disabled young man sitting on the front row. His attentiveness and response drew me to him. Afterwards he stayed to speak. When I asked about his physical condition he said, "Mr. Smith, I have a handicap; the handicap doesn't have me."

In the years of physical deterioration, I have been tempted to fall prey to the black cloud. I daily make decisions about my attitude.

My Son, My Son

I constantly work to focus on the things I have, not on the things I don't. Guideposts magazine quoted me when I said, "I am not disabled - I am delightfully dependent."

Recently, a friend told me he stayed home rather than fight the inclement weather. This meant he didn't get his gym time. So, he stretched out on the floor to exercise. Only then did he realize how beautiful the ceilings were in their house. He could have been out of sorts for missing his scheduled workout, but he let gratitude work in his heart.

There are certainly clinical reasons for depression that require medical attention. I am not minimizing those.

A therapist told me one of the cures for non-clinical depression is getting outside ourselves and giving to others. "Grateful people are usually generous." This leads us to see gratitude as a shield against the fiery darts of despair."

Wes had things in his life to be depressed about. We all do. As the days go by there seems to be more and more reasons to be despondent. Without Christ that is surely true. With Christ, we are called to live in hope. When we have that hope, gratitude becomes possible. My journey through grief has truly been lightened as I practiced gratefulness.

Wes and I often talked about what we were grateful for. I found the following in his journals/prayers:

March 22, 2007 from Journal
Lord, thank You for carrying me—help me to know when you are and to relax in Your arms. Amen

August 12, 2010
He who is grateful can see the good things of this world with clear eyes. Be thankful for what you can see as well as what you can't see. Remain in an on-going act of thanksgiving.

Gratitude

> August 8, 2010
> To be completely honest, I've never had a true need that wasn't met!

What especially blessed me about Fred's thoughts was the link between gratitude and generosity. "Grateful people are usually generous." Some of the last written words in Wes' journals were about generosity.

> August 9, 2010
> Christians are to be the most generous. How am I doing at being generous? Why is it that greed bankrupts but generosity doesn't?

His last written prayer in his journals:

> September 13, 2010
> Lord, Help me to be the most generous I can be to others.
> Amen

And to that I can only say Amen to that! God granted that prayer. My son, my son, you lived with a generous, loving spirit!

My Son, My Son

Epilogue

"Miss Evelyn, your boy, he at the house." Denver kindly comforted me when I told him about my son's death. My wound was fresh and his words were like balm. Denver was a formerly homeless black man who was very wise. He became a writer, speaker, and a friend to me and my husband. Www.samekindofdifferentasme.com His words remain as among the most comforting of all I heard over the years. As a mother you always worry that your child will make it home safely. The ultimate safety is arriving in Heaven.

In Wes' journal from 5-23-09:

> "When trouble comes, think about how many things God has given you. The memory of the gift can temper the pain of affliction and the foreboding and fear of affliction can modify the joy of the gift. (Be) pure of heart. To be near God is my refuge."

I have come to realize that I think more and more of my son with gratitude instead of pain. I remember the first moment I saw him in the hospital when he was born. I looked into his sweet baby face and knew he was a gift from God. He provided so much joy to my life. He helped me grow as a person. He fulfilled much of what I wanted out of life…to have a child that I could love. He grew up to be a kind and caring man. Not only was he my beloved son, but he was also a true Christian and friend.

As I stay near to God, He helps bring the good memories back to me. We are all here on earth only for a short time. I want to live the rest of my life being grateful and generous to others. I don't want to waste another minute being depressed and sidelined. I want to tell the story of my son not only to warn about the psychiatric drugs but also to comfort others. I want to see God bring good out of tragedy and use my costly training in grief.

If you have also experienced grief, I can tell you there is reason for encouragement. Comfort is available! God's love transforms.

God has mercifully shown His love to me through the gift of my son and carrying me through my grief. I pray that I can share what I know for sure about His love and comfort. Yes, Wes is at the house. Denver is there and my mother and countless loved ones. I plan to take every opportunity I can to share God's love until I am finally also, "at the house."

About The Author

Evelyn Hinds is a speaker and author. She is the founder of Arts Touching Hearts, Inc., a ministry committed to expressing the message of God through the arts. She is a spokesperson for the Corrie ten Boom House and Museum in Holland. In addition to speaking and writing, she performs a one woman show as Corrie.

Additional copies of this book are available at http://www.amazon.com/.

To contact Evelyn or to order her first book called "The Weaving" email her at evelyn@evelynhinds.com.

Evelyn's website is www.evelynhinds.com.